Advance Praise for
The Power Principles of Time Mastery

Walt Hampton doesn't waste your time with this book… short, sweet and powerful.

> — Steve Chandler, author of
> *Reinventing Yourself*

This powerful book uncovers the simple truths of happiness, results and better performance in business and life.

> — JT DeBolt, author of
> *Flight Plan to Success*

Bright, breezy, and beautifully beneficial. Crazy busy? Go all-in to master your time.

> — Robert Vanourek, author of
> *Triple Crown Leadership*

Your time is the most important resource you will ever have, yet only if you cherish it. Walt Hampton makes so much swift sense, you might just change your whole life, in just minutes per day.

> — Tama Kieves, bestselling author of
> *Inspired & Unstoppable: Wildly*
> *Succeeding in Your Life's Work!* and
> *A Year Without Fear: 365 Days*
> *of Magnificence*

I used to consider myself the time guru. Then I read Walt's book. If you want to do something smart, buy this book and do just what he says. Walt knows time like Buddha knows peace.

— Dr. Bridget Cooper, author of
Feed the Need

The practical genius of Walt Hampton's *Time Mastery* system in three words: Simple. Fun. Effective. Seize the power of *Time Mastery* and watch your impact, fulfillment and life transform before your eyes.

— Matthew Cross, Founder
& President, Leadership Alliance
bestselling author of
*The Golden Ratio of Da Vinci,
Fibonacci & You*

The Power Principles of

Time Mastery

Do Less. Make More. Have Fun.

Walt Hampton, J.D.

Summit Press Publishers

Power Principles of Time Mastery
Do Less. Make More. Have Fun.
By Walt Hampton, J.D.

Copyright © 2015

Published by

Summit Press

Summit Press Publishers
Canton, Connecticut
860-306-4057 Phone
860-281-2750 Fax
www.summit-success.com

Cover Design and Interior Design by Summit Press

ISBN: 978-0-692-20710-9

Second Edition, 2015

First Edition, 2014
Published in the United States of America

Making contact with the author for speaking, coaching, consulting or ordering large book quantities is hassle free. Simply reach out to Walt at walt@walthampton.com

It is in the moments of decision that your destiny is shaped.

Anthony Robbins

For Ann, my running partner, climbing partner, business partner, wife and very best friend.

I am blessed to spend my time with you.

Contents

Foreword

This book will change your life. Or not. It depends. If you're like me, you've probably said,

*"I just don't have the time to
(fill-in the blank with: exercise, read for pleasure,
take that vacation, go to a ball game with a friend, …)."*

Virtually every time I said that, I was wrong. And you, all too often, are wrong too. Of course you have time to (fill in the blank again). You *choose* not to because of the frenetic, harried world we live in, sometimes by necessity because of the circumstances you are in, but oftentimes by choice. Like me, you prioritized other activities over what you chose not to do. We need to stop making those bad choices.

It takes discipline, commitment, practice, and courage to change your life through the conscious choices you make. And unless you are quite disciplined and creative, a wise guide will help you immensely. Walt Hampton can be that guide.

In this powerful, little book, rich with stories, funny and deep, Walt will show you how to change your life for the better. Walt is an expert at living life to its fullest. I admire him immensely and wish he had been my guide long ago. I would be a better person today.

Walt is an inspirational set of intriguing contradictions. He's a master motivator who mindfully meditates. He bounces between homes in Connecticut and Castletownshend, Ireland. He's been a tenacious litigator and is now a dream-catcher.

Walt loves to live on life's edge. He is a wiry ice and rock climber and ski-mountaineer. He's ivy-trained and an accomplished photographer from craggy mountaintops to cows crossing roads. He's a long-distance runner, pilot, scuba diver, and sailor. Whew.

When speaking to audiences, Walt can mesmerize you, as he has me while I sat in the audience and listened to him spin his adventure stories with that infuriatingly infectious grin on his face, a bundle of high-octane energy in action. I love to follow Walt's Facebook posts. The quotes are so spot-on and the pictures make you laugh and shake your head, or marvel at the awe he captures while out on a run or climbing some peak I've never heard of.

Walt is an audacious explorer of both nature and souls. He tells it as it needs to be told, and his genuine optimism radiates out and touches your heart. What an incredible guide you have on these powerful pages.

You should also know Walt Hampton has spent time on dark side too: divorced and the single dad of three boisterous boys, he somehow juggled a highly successful and demanding legal practice for decades, searching all the while for a new soul mate whom he has finally found in his co-adventurer and co-conspirator, Ann Sheybani (her story and quest is another fascinating tale).

> *How do we balance it all in life?*
> *What should we choose to do?*
> *What should we choose not to do?*
> *How can we master what can't be mastered:*
> *the unforgiving, relentless ticks of time?*

We can't manage time of course, but we can manage ourselves, our choices, so much better, avoiding those never-to-be-retrieved, black holes that suck away our precious daily seconds.

Walt shows us how to:

- Simplify, doing less so we can do more
- Focus with crystal clarity on what's really important
- Define our life's true purpose
- Build good fences for fair boundaries
- Create "free zones" where interruptions and addictive habits are verboten
- Artfully say "No," gaining respectful admiration in the process

- Set smart goals
- Practice what he preaches

Time Mastery is rich with practical tools from planner templates to values exercises, a thought-provoking "Wheel of Life," and inspirational quotes from his incredible network of friends. Walt's quick-read pages will inspire you to stop the excuses and decisively commit to go *"all in,"* as he has, to change your life.

Walt coaches executives, leaders, and just-us folks around the world, optimistically tweaking the noses of their choices, delighting in playing the maverick, bravely asking the questions we should be asking ourselves, but just don't. Now Walt's wonderful wisdom has been distilled into this treasure of power principles.

How you spend your time will determine your life and your legacy.

Will you be remembered as that crazy-busy, frantic, frenetic person running from pillar to post, multi-tasking everything, spinning out of control, letting life drive you?

Or will you be admired as the master of your time, living a life that matters with true joy, purpose and passion, mindful and wise with places of sanctuary, and driving your life where you choose to go?

This book will change your life. Or not. It depends on the choices you will make. Choose wisely. Your life depends on it.

Bob Vanourek

Former CEO of five companies and co-author of *Triple Crown Leadership: Building Excellent, Ethical, and Enduring Organizations*, a 2013 International Book award winner

January 2015

Introduction

I've got some bad news and some good news.

The bad news is that there isn't any more of "it."

The good news is that you've got *all* there is. No one has any more of it than you. *You've got it all.*

Time.

"I have no time."

"There's never enough time in the day."

"Where has the time gone?"

Everyone wants to "manage" time. Time, however, is not amenable to management. In fact, it can't be managed. It's made up. It's just a construct. It just is.

But... and this is more good news... you *can* manage you. And when you can do that, you will master time.

I had to master time the hard way.

I was a single dad for a dozen years, raising three young boys on my own, while managing a law firm and trying to stay sane. This is how most of my days would unfold: The alarm would go off at 6:30 a.m., I'd stumble down for a cup of coffee, wake the boys for school, make the school lunches, wake the boys up again, shower and get dressed for work, mediate the arguments, help find the lost socks, and the homework, make the breakfasts, pack the backpacks, tear off to daycare and to school, drop off the kids, run to the office, pick up the files for court, get stuck in traffic, get to court just barely on time, get the call from daycare that the youngest had a 102° fever or head lice (again) or both, run back to the office to pick up my files, retrieve the sick kid, work at my kitchen counter, juggling emails and phone conferences, scheduling and re-scheduling appointments and depositions and court appearances, get the snacks ready for the older kids when they got home from school, unpack the backpacks, hear about the day, mediate the fights, run off to soccer practice or baseball practice or lacrosse practice (or all of them), rush home to make dinner (hopefully not out of a can again), mediate the fights, help with the homework, run out to Staples™ for the poster board for the project that's due tomorrow, finish the homework, mediate the fights, read the stories, put the kids to bed, return the calls, answer the emails, stagger to bed, fall into a fitful sleep; and then wake up the next day to do it all over again.

Yes, I know a few things about time.

If you're suffering a time famine, if you'd like to "find" some more time, you are not alone. I work with business leaders, professionals, executives, managers, artists and entrepreneurs from all over the world. Nearly everyone struggles with how to accomplish it all, how to fit it all in, how to get it all done… and not feel like a burned out hulk at the end of the day.

But, thankfully, you don't have to be "everyone," you don't have to struggle. And you certainly don't have to learn this stuff the hard way. I've developed a set of principles – power principles – that if applied will make you much more productive; you'll have a lot less stress in your life, and a whole lot more joy.

You'll have the time.

Let me show you how.

How To Use This Book

Time is not linear. (We'll talk about that later!) And how you use this book doesn't have to be linear either. It's full of tools, tips, and strategies. You can read it straight through... or jump around.

There are also some templates and exercises at the back of the book that I think you'll find helpful. When you come to a place in the book that references one of the templates, don't feel as if you absolutely need to jump there right away... unless you simply can't wait!

But here's what's really important: If you really want to have a saner life, don't just read this book. Use it. Apply the principles. The application of even one or two of them will switch up the entire game and make your life sweeter.

Think how fast the last week has flown by. Or the last year. You only get one shot at this thing called your life.

Become a master of your time.

Chapter 1
Do Less

Yes, that's right. Do less. That's Power Principle #1.

Now I know that sounds like a ridiculous place to start. After all, isn't the point of time "management" the ability to get more done?

NO! That's not the point. The point is to be able to pay attention to the really important stuff in your life… and to enjoy it all a whole lot more along the way.

Culturally, of course, this flies in the face of everything we've been taught. We're taught that in order to succeed, we need to work longer, harder, faster; that every moment counts; that every moment of our day needs to be productive; that time is money; and that wasting time is tantamount to flushing money down the drain.

Busy has become a weird badge of honor.

I'll see a colleague at the post office and ask, "How are you?"

"Busy," comes the reply… with a wry smile and a stern, knowing nod of the head.

Or, "Crazy busy," with the word crazy drawn out to sound like this: craaaaaaaaaazy.

As if the busier we are, the more important we are, or the more significant our work.

As if the craaaaaazier we are, the more we're getting done.

Which is just the opposite of the truth. The truth is: The busier we are, the less we're really accomplishing in our lives. The busier we are, the more we're like hamsters on a wheel. The busier we are, the more empty and depleted we become.

Busy is bad.

Busy means that we're paying way too much attention to the urgent; and far too little attention to what really matters.

Busy means that the circumstances of life have mastered us; and that we are not masters of our time.

That we are not masters of ourselves.

Now, when I see a colleague at the post office and hear "Busy," I say, "Oh, I'm so sorry to hear that." As if they've just told me that someone has died. Which elicits a strange and quizzical look.

Which, of course, is good. Because we all need to do less.

By doing less, we have greater focus, deeper reserves and higher resiliency.

Less is more. It really is.

You'll see.

Chapter 2
On A Clear Day

Ok, you say, maybe it would feel good to be a little less craaaaazy. Maybe I'd really like to be a little less busy; maybe it might actually open up a little more time.

But I've got a lot to do! A lot of people depend on me! A lot of people are expecting a ton of work from me! How in God's name do I get there?

Well it starts with getting clear about what's really important to you. Absolutely crystal clear.

When I was growing up, my dad was a physician, a GP. My mom stayed at home. There were seven of us kids. It was pretty craaaaazy.

We lived in a small town in New England, across the street from the Catholic Church. My mom was a devout Irish Catholic.

When my dad would get home at the end of the day, he'd be pretty spent. There was always a lot of noise in the house. And when we'd sit down for dinner, the scene resembled something like piranha feeding in a river of slain cows.

My father did not suffer fools; and at the end of the day he had little or no patience. He would become especially annoyed when the phone would ring during dinner; and a ringing phone would cause him to erupt more times than not.

I remember one evening sitting down to dinner when my dad was in an especially cantankerous mood. The phone rang. He jumped up from the table, ripped the phone out of the cradle and yelled into the receiver: "Who are you and what the hell do you want?"

There was silence.

My dad looked at my mom. And then stretched the handset over to her saying, "It's Father Shea. He wants to talk with you about the altar guild."

A funny story that I'll never forget.

But critically important questions that each one of us needs to ask and answer for ourselves.

Who are you?

And what the hell do you want?

What are you called to do in this world? What's your vision? What's your mission? What's most important to you? What do you most want in this life? What impact do you want to make in the world? What do you want to leave behind? What do you want your legacy to be?

The answers to these questions begin with what you value.

What do you really, really value... not what do you think you "should" value; or what society says you "should" value; or what your family or your friends tell you that you "should" value. But rather, deep in your heart... what is it that you value most in the world?

One way to get to the nub of this pretty quickly is to think about your eulogy. Yeah, you'll "be" there but not likely in the way you'd want to be.

Fast forward to that moment. What will folks be saying about you? (What do you want folks to be saying about you?) About your values? About your impact? They likely won't be talking about the number of hours you billed last year or how much is in your bank account or how many "units" you sold, or how great your Power Point™ slides were, or how many of your kid's soccer games you missed because you were out of town on the road doing deals, or how many LinkedIn contacts you had.

At the end of our lives what will be important will be the relationships we've formed, the experiences we've had, the love that we've shared. What will matter will be whether we've lived richly, fully, deeply and without regret.

Usually, when looked at through this lens, it's not terribly complicated to figure out what we really value. Usually it's about what brings us joy and meaning. And usually what brings us joy and meaning is pretty damn simple. Things like connecting with family and friends; our homes; a sunrise; our garden; the first snow; our health and wellness; the time and space to breathe.

For me it's my fitness; my connection with my wife, Ann; my little cottage retreat in Ireland; and the time to read and write.

What are the things you value? Write them down!

And… here's where the rubber meets the road: Are you "doing" what you value?

Here's a little exercise: Get out a blank sheet of paper. Hold it landscape-wise. Draw a line down the middle. Now in the left hand column, list the top 5 things you value; in the right hand column, list the top 5 places where you spend your time.

You'll find a template for this in the back of the book on page 64.

Now, here's what's interesting. In the ideal world, there would be a 1:1 correlation between the two columns; you spend your time on what you value.

But, more often than not, that's not the case. There's incongruity. We aren't spending our time on what we value.

We say that we value fitness, and yet we never spend time in the gym; we say we value family, and yet we spend 80 hours a week in the office. We say we value life-long learning, and yet we haven't spent time with a book in years.

Now, there's no particular problem with one column or the other. The problem is the discord.

Once we get clear on what we value, it becomes much easier to see how we might become less busy.

We can actually do less and focus more on the stuff that really, truly matters.

Chapter 3
Good Fences

If you stopped right here and read no further, your life would be forever changed. If you were to live each day through the lens of your eulogy, filtering each decision, each commitment, each moment of time through those things you value most, you would make decisions about how you spend your time in a vastly different way.

But, of course, understanding a concept and actually applying it can be "challenging." So let's consider some practical tools.

Robert Frost once wrote, "Good fences make good neighbors." With good fences – clearer boundaries – you'll be a better neighbor to yourself. Becoming good at setting boundaries is one of the best ways to become a master of your time.

No doubt you make lists… you likely wouldn't be someone reading this book if you weren't. But I bet you probably haven't made a "stop doing" list; a list of things that you will NOT be doing.

You see, most of us construct long lists of things we need to do. But there are a whole lot of things in our lives that we shouldn't be doing. We like to pretend that we have control over these things. And yet, we're so often drawn into a web of stuff that we promised ourselves "last time" that we wouldn't do again. Like taking on yet another term on that charity board, doing the room parent gig again, chairing the fund raiser for the soccer league for the sixth year in a row, going to that blasted networking event that has never yielded a single lead, or spending yet another holiday at your sister's house, yeah the one who always criticizes you.

Things that we've done in the past that we're tired of, worn out from; events we've gone to that are boring or haven't worked out well; relationships that haven't nurtured us or have, in fact, brought us down.

Maybe you've heard of the Pareto Principle.

Vilfredo Pareto was an Italian economist who observed that 80% of the land in Italy was owned by 20% of the people. He found this to be true in other countries as well.

At home in his garden, Pareto discovered that 20% of his pea pods yielded 80% of the peas.

Pareto was intrigued. Over time, this principle, now known as The Pareto Principle or the 80/20 Rule, has been found to apply to many areas across the spectrum of business, sales, technology, healthcare, education… and in many areas of daily living.

- For example, and you'll know this to be true, 80% of your sales come from 20% of your clients
- And 80% of your headaches come from 20% of your clients!
- 80% of profits come from 20% of staff time expended
- 80% of sales are made by 20% of staff
- 80% of profits come from 20% of products
- In industry, 20% of the hazards cause 80% of the injuries
- In healthcare, 20% of patients use 80% of the resources

Applied liberally (and ruthlessly), 20% of your efforts yield 80% of your outcomes.

IF this is TRUE (and IT IS!), why not just get rid of the 80%?

Take a close look at your life. There are a bunch of things that are not "high yield" endeavors. There are activities that have gotten "old." There are relationships that don't serve you.

Make a list of those things that you are not going to do anymore. This is your "Stop Doing List." Post it prominently. Review it daily.

You'll find a template for your list in the back of the book on page 65.

Chapter 4
Just Say No

Now with your values firmly in mind and your Stop Doing List clearly delineated, you know what you want… and what you don't want. You know what activities give you the "biggest bang for your buck" and which ones are soul-sucking black holes.

It's time to say no.

You've got a work project you love and a sick kid at home. You get asked to bake for the holiday party (again). You need to say no.

There's a client who wants to retain you again. He was "high maintenance," and that last engagement was a nightmare. You need to say no.

You've chaired the historical commission for the last three years. "No one else can do it like you." But you're tired of the work, you've got a newborn at home, and you haven't been to the gym in a decade. You need to say no.

Your mother-in-law wants you to come for Thanksgiving for the fifth year in a row. Every year, her brother gets drunk and picks a fight with you. You've got to say no.

By saying no to what isn't working in our lives, we can say yes to what is. By saying no, we open up time for ourselves, we create space. We reclaim sanity. By saying no we also create opportunities for others to step up and serve in ways that perhaps they never would have done.

When I was a single dad running a law practice, I had to get good at saying no. I had to say no to late afternoon meetings and depositions; I had to say no to judges who wanted me to appear on days that there were important school activities; I had to say no to clients who wanted to meet me in the evening.

Now, of course, there's an "art" to saying no. It feels good to be asked to do something. It feeds our ego, our need for significance, our desire to connect and make a contribution. So you don't want to toss off the request haphazardly. You want to affirm the relationship. You want to acknowledge, with gratitude, the fact that you were asked. You also want to suggest alternatives for the person asking, *e.g.*, "Have you considered asking David to chair that committee? He'd be great at that." But you want to be decisive, clear and unequivocal

Here's what I've learned: When we're crystal clear about what we value most, when we know what's working in our lives and what's not, it becomes much easier to say no. And when we say no from that place of integrity, the world is kinder to us.

Never in a dozen years of juggling my parenting needs with my law practice did I ever get challenged or treated badly. Because, what's also true is that when we say no from this place, we give permission to others to say no as well. And all of us want more sanity; all of us want better fences, clearer boundaries.

Do the things that reflect what you value most, that serve your mission, that light up your life, that provide the highest and best return for you and for those you love. Say no to the rest.

And if you find yourself saying that "this is something I 'should' do," take that as a warning. You probably shouldn't!

Create good boundaries through the art of saying no, and your life will become much sweeter.

Chapter 5
Orlando or San Francisco?

Unless you have nothing better to do with your time, you likely wouldn't show up at the American Airlines ticket counter this afternoon and say, "Gimme a ticket; I don't care where to." The rep would probably give you a funny look and tell you that you needed to decide; you had to choose a destination.

Indeed, when you go off on a trip, you usually have a pretty clear idea where you're going and how you're going to get there. You've mapped out the route and booked your hotels.

Even in your daily life, when you're driving about, you likely know how to get to your office, your dentist's office, your local movie theater, your favorite restaurant, and your home. There are clear, defined, known routes you follow to clear, known, defined destinations.

But what's interesting is that many times we show up in our work, at our job, on a project or in our life without any clear idea at all about where we want to end up or how we're going to get there. We just kind of wander. And in the wandering, not much gets done at all. We end up at the end of the day, the end of the week, the end of the year wondering where the time went and why we didn't get much done.

It's because we didn't start off with the destination in mind.

When we're growing up and going to school, there's a path we follow, a defined (by others) trajectory. And the destination has been pre-ordained: Graduation, college, graduate school, advanced degree, job, career. But many times, after we've gotten out of school and into "real" life, we find that there's no "curriculum," per se, and there's a propensity for aimless wandering to set in.

But we still get to choose.

What do you want to accomplish with your life? What are your big life goals? When you look back on your life, what do you want to have achieved?

How about in the next year? What do you want to get done? What projects will you have completed? What difference will you have made? You know, only a small percentage of the population even bothers to make New Year's resolutions any more, so jaded we have become about our ability to effect change even in our own lives.

What about in the week ahead? When you fall into bed at the end of the week, will you look back and say, "Wow, I made so much progress toward my cherished dreams!" Or will you lay there in the dark frustrated that yet another week of your precious life has slid by without getting to those things that really matter to you?

How about today? Do you know exactly what you're going to do today?

Where do you want to end up?

And what do you want the outcome to be?

Choose your destination.

Chapter 6
What's Your Why?

A ll right, good on you if you're clear on where you want to go. But, do you know *why* you want to get there?

Without a clear "why," getting to your destination will be tough. You'll "waste" a lot of time with hand wringing and uncertainty.

These are some of the refrains I hear from my coaching clients:

"I've hit a plateau with my sales."

"Organizing the office space is just too overwhelming."

"I can't seem to get the grant proposal done."

"I just don't have enough time to finish the book."

"The weight just won't come off."

All of us have places where we seem to hit a wall; where we get stymied; where it seems that we just can't bust through.

It's usually *not* about a "time management" problem.

It's usually because we're not clear about our "why."

Angelo was frustrated. Try as he did to bring in more mortgage loan originations, none of his warm leads panned out. It was as if the Midas touch he once had had turned everything to coal.

Angelo was one of my high-performance coaching clients. He knew all the success tools; all the strategies. And he knew how to execute; he was someone who took action.

But when I asked him "why" it was that he wanted to boost his numbers, he faltered. He already made a fair amount of money; so it wasn't just about the comp. He already had a lot of freedom and flexibility; so it wasn't about the time. He already was pretty senior in the company; so it wasn't about position or prestige.

So I dug a bit…. It turned out that Angelo had never been able to take his wife on a honeymoon; and despite the passage of nearly a dozen years of marriage and much success, Angelo still wanted to surprise his wife with a trip to Italy. As soon as he focused on this "why," his numbers soared.

Without the "why," a task is just a task… yet another item on an endless list of interminable "to dos."

Take the recyclables to the curb… Check.

Make the cold call… Check.

Stop for milk on the way home… Check.

One chore no more important than the next.

The list will wear us down. **It is the "why" that lights us up.**

Our vision, our "why," is the North Star. It shines in the darkness; it guides us through our desert wastelands.

It is what excites us and sustains us; it is the fuel that drives us forward.

Author and coach Dan Sullivan writes, **"Having a purpose that is greater than yourself will give you a constant impetus to strive."**

Simon Sinek says, "Start with why." **"Those who know their why are the ones who lead,"** he says. **"They are the ones who inspire."**

The most successful people on the planet have a vision of where they're going… *and why they want to get there.* Even in the littlest of things.

So dig until you find your "why."

Because when you know your "why," you will find the how.

And then you are **unstoppable.**

Definiteness of purpose is the starting point of all achievement.

W. Clement Stone

Chapter 7
Have A Plan

Ok, so now you know that time mastery starts out with getting clear on what you really want. You need a clear vision. And a compelling "why."

You need specific goals; you need a target, a destination.

Now you need a map; and a plan for following the map.

Jim Rohn once said, "If you don't design your own life plan, chances are you'll fall into someone else's plan. And guess what they have planned for you? Not much."

You must have a plan: for your day, for your week, for your month, for your life.

When I want to go off on a mountain climbing expedition, after I've picked my (precise) summit, I plan. I pick the best route. I study the route description. I look at photos of the route. I study the weather to consider the best time of year to make the climb. I decide how much time the route will take me. And I set aside the time. I choose my equipment and my clothing and I check it all carefully to be sure it's in top condition. I plan out my food and determine exactly how much fuel I'll need for the cook stoves. I meet with my team to discuss the route and the contingencies. And then I start.

Without this level of planning, we could get into trouble, get off route, run out of food, jeopardize our safety, lose our lives.

This is the level of detail we should have in our day-to-day lives. Otherwise, we will run out of time… all of it.

It all starts with a map.

Let's think about this like one of those GPS units you have in your car.

Your destination is what you plug in. It's where you want to end up. But before your GPS spits out your route in that sexy mechanical voice, it needs another piece of information: where you are right now.

You want to know exactly where you are.

My mentor Tony Robbins says that we want to see things as they are; not worse than they are; not better than they are. But as they really are. Because it is only with that level of clarity that we can chart our course with certainly. If we delude ourselves that we are in a different place or discourage ourselves with the false beliefs about our circumstances, we'll use up a lot of time in futile efforts.

I remember a trail my wife and I were going to explore.

We looked at the map. We studied the topo. We were pretty psyched.

Our plan was to run twelve miles along the ridgeline. It would be our first trail-run in the training program for our ultra marathon.

We started in the pre-dawn light. For a while, the route followed a level, well-traveled path. Then the trail cut uphill steeply and disappeared into the brush. Several times we needed to turn around to get back on route. Several times we needed to stop to figure out which way to go. The trail was marked with blue blazes – but not very well.

Along the way, we got lost. It was hot and buggy. We fell. We got up again.

And when we were finished, we were well pleased with our success.

We started with a map.

Most of us do when we're planning a hike in the woods. Or a road trip.

But it's astounding how few of us use a map for the rest of our lives.

Of course, we start out with good intentions, and a general idea of the direction: stay in school, get good grades, find a job, get married, settle down, work hard, make money. Then you'll be happy. You'll get "there," wherever "there" is supposed to be.

The problem is: the path peters out. It gets hot and buggy. There aren't enough markers. We lose our way. We can't even begin to remember where "there" might be.

And without a map, we're screwed.

But here's the good news: *We* are the cartographers! We get to draw the map! We get to plot the course!

We are the architects of our lives.

Sure stuff happens. Bad things do happen to good people. We do get off course. We do lose our way. There is sickness and suffering and death. But as Viktor Frankl wrote in his magnificent masterpiece, *Man's Search for Meaning*, even in the worst of circumstances, *we get to choose.*

And it is our responsibility to choose.

It is our responsibility to be active participants in the gift of our lives, to be drivers and not passengers. What a privilege it is to be able to step up and chart out our own course; to choose our own way.

We can drift along, let things happen, see how things turn out. Many folks do. But usually those are the folks we hear complaining about how horrible the economy is, how unfair the pay is, how mean the boss is, how they're getting screwed at every turn.

The alternative is to draw the map.

So chart the course:

- What are your dreams?
- What is the life you want?
- Who would be your ideal partner?
- How do you envision your health?
- Where do you want to live?
- What do you want your net worth to be?
- What kind of work would rock your world?

Write it down. Map it out. And start out.

Make it happen. Sometimes, we'll go back to the drawing board. And yes, we'll still get lost and fall down and get hurt.

But we'll have a map.

Chapter 8
Get Smart

S ometimes we're smart; most of the time we're not.

We're most often smart when we know we're taking a trip to Paris; or we want the executive director's position; or we're going to run the fall half-marathon.

We're not terribly smart when we want our marriage to be better or we want to get healthier or we'd like a new career.

Let me explain.

Goals can be like cotton candy. They look delightful; gooey, sticky, sweet. We go at them with a vengeance; and then we end up with a discouraging stomachache promising that we'll never ever do "that" again.

Or goals can be like a Star Trek transporter delivering us on a laser beam of light to a wondrous destination.

Of course, like anything, we get to choose how we want our goals to be. I want to suggest that, as time masters, you make your goals smart. As in S.M.A.R.T.

The "S" stands for specific. Your goals need to be clear, defined and specific in order to be attained efficiently. For example, you might look at your sorry old fat self in the mirror on New Year's Eve and decide that you're finally ready to "do" something. You could make your resolution like this: "I'm going to get healthier next year; yup, next year is going to be different; I'm going to be healthier."

Or, you could make your goal this: "Next year I'm going to lose 30 pounds."

Which goal are you more likely to attain without wasting your precious time?

The goal that is specific.

Ok, the "M" stands for measureable. Your goals, to be effective, need to be measureable goals; they need to have readily accessible metrics; you need to be able to regularly and accurately assess your progress.

Let's stick with the New Year's resolution of getting healthier. How are you measuring healthier? When you stand in the mirror next New Year's Eve, how will you know if you're healthier? By how you "look," or how you "feel?" Or will you know because your cholesterol has dropped by 20 points, or your blood pressure; or you've gone from a size 8 to a size 4?

Dan Ariely writing in the Harvard Business Review says, "Human beings adjust behavior based on the metrics they're held against. Anything you measure will impel a person to optimize his score on that metric. What you measure is what you'll get. Period."

If you want to succeed at your goal in a reasonable period of time, measure; apply the "M."

An attainable goal also needs to be actionable. If you were to say, "I'd like to be younger," that's not a goal you can take action on (with all due respect to Ponce de Leon). If you were to say, I want to get healthier, then you're getting closer. And if you say, I want to lose 30 pounds, well, now you're on to something you can take concrete action on. That's a specific goal; it's a goal you can measure every day; and every day you can do something that will get you closer to that goal.

The "R" stands for realistic. Your goal needs to be something you can reasonably attain. There's nothing that will throw us faster into a heap of despair than discouragement. You don't want to set yourself up for failure.

As a coach, I believe that anything is possible. If you want to have a six or seven figure income, you can have that. But if you're starting off in a brand new enterprise, it may not be realistic... at least not in the first year.

So going back to the weight loss example, let's say you're looking in that mirror at your side spludge and decide that you need to lose 100 pounds. Now that may be true. And it certainly is specific. And you can certainly measure it. But it might not be a realistically achievable goal this year.

Make your goals realistic goals and you will be much less likely to get discouraged along the way. There's no greater waste of time than to start off, throw in the towel, then show back up next year in that mirror only to have to start all over again.

Finally, have a "T," a time deadline. Make your goals time bound, time specific.

I'll tell you as a distance runner, there's nothing more compelling for me than to have a race date looming. That keeps me moving forward!

And a coach once told me, when I was just thinking about launching my speaking career, "Do something to make it inevitable." When I asked what, he said, "Book a date to speak."

Well, I did; even before I had come up with a speech. And that certainly lit the fire!

So maybe you want to lose that 30 pounds before your high school reunion on September 15; or fit into that gown for your daughter's wedding on June 1; or be able to run that half marathon on October 10. Whatever it is, put a "T" on it. The deadline will compel you to a masterful use of your time!

Get smart; be smart; stay smart.

Chapter 9
Carnegie Hall

Remember the old riddle, "What's the fastest way to Carnegie Hall?" Answer: "Practice."

Practice matters. Discipline matters.

Mastery is about showing up every day. Doing the work. Putting in the 10,000 hours.

The same is true with time mastery. If you want to become a master of time, you need to actually do it.

It needs to become a practice, a habit; something you don't re-think every day; something you just do. It needs to be hard-wired; dialed in.

I want to suggest some efficient time mastery practices.

Let's start with weekly planning. That's the easiest place of entry. There's a template for this in the back of the book on page 66.

On a Saturday or a Sunday, carve out an hour of time. Just for your time mastery.

Now, I don't want to hear your complaining and moaning that you "don't have the time" to do this. You don't have the time NOT to do this. (And besides, we've already concluded that you likely have enough extra time to paint the Sistine Chapel all over again.) This work is like the prep work you do for a painting or wallpapering job. Once the prep work is done, the project is easy. This hour you set aside to do your weekly planning is worth 100 times your investment in this book; it's worth its weight in gold; it will make all the difference in your life. So no skimping. Your first order of business is to carve out an hour. Define it. Schedule it. Make it happen. No matter what.

In this hour, the very first step is to close your eyes, and imagine the week ahead going exactly like you want it to go; everything unfolding perfectly, just like you want it to be.

Maybe last week was crazy; maybe last week was chaotic; how do you want this week to go?

What is the *experience* you want this week? How do you want it to *feel?* Write down what you want your experiences to be! These experiences will anchor you; and will provide you with the emotional framework for your week ahead. Don't skip this step.

Now ask yourself, what are the concrete results that you want to create this week? What are the big-ticket game-changers that you want to accomplish? What are those things, that if you came to the end of the week, you would feel frustrated about if you hadn't accomplished them? What are the significant, specific results that will advance you toward your big goals, your life vision? Write these down.

Ok, now into the actual nitty gritty: We're going to look at each of the major areas of your life: Financial, Career and Business, Health & Wellness, Personal, Relationships, your Spiritual and Emotional life, and your Community Contribution.

I won't belabor this by plodding through each area. But let's do one or two to give you the idea, to get you going.

Let's pick Health & Wellness for example. First, before you dive into the concrete results you'd like to create in this area during the week ahead, I want you to get associated with the experiences again. What do you want to experience in this area of health and wellness in the week ahead? Increased energy? Increased vitality? Youthful exuberance? Ease of movement? Whatever these experiences are, experience them, taste them… and then write them down. Because, again it will be the experiences you attach to the result that will provide you with the momentum to go the distance.

All right, so now we have the experience you want to have of health & wellness, what are the particular results you want to create? A loss of 1 pound? (I use this example purposefully… so often folks forget even in this process to make their weekly goals SMART goals… they're not realistic in light of their own personal history… but here, a pound a week is pretty realistic… and over a year yields more than 50 pounds!) Here's another result: get to the gym three times this week. Or take in two yoga classes. Or try out a fitness coach. Or maybe it's to get a new vegetarian cookbook. Write down those specific results.

Now, and here's the key: go over to your planner, your day timer, your Outlook or gCal, whatever you use (you *have* to use a planner; it's not an option if you want mastery) AND actually schedule in when you are going to do these things. Schedule in the gym time; schedule in the yoga time; schedule the time you'll go online to choose the cookbook; schedule your weigh-ins if the loss of weight is a goal (and while I'm on it, schedule in exactly how many calories you'll consume each day to get this result.)

I can't emphasize this scheduling piece enough. If it's not actually scheduled in – like a real live commitment, it will fall off the plate; it won't happen. Ensure that you'll get this result by actually scheduling in the time.

You don't blow off a dentist appointment or a client meeting that's scheduled... you just wouldn't do that. It's on the calendar. Give the same import to your own goals!

Let's take another area as an example: Let's go with Relationships.

Start again with the experiences you want to create. Maybe it's a feeling of closeness with your spouse; maybe it's a deeper friendship; maybe it's a sense of deepening connection with a child or a parent. Whatever it is, feel it. And then describe it in writing on your weekly plan.

Next, write down the results you want to create. Is it a date night with a partner or spouse? Is it a magic moment with a child? Is it a glass of wine or a cup of coffee with an old friend? Write down the specific results, outcomes, goals.

And now – this is key - go to your calendar... NOW... and SCHEDULE it! Put it in writing ON THE CALENDAR.

So this is a three-step process. And each step is really important. FIRST, get tuned in to and identified with the EXPERIENCES you would like to have in each of the major areas of your life in the week ahead; SECOND, write down the SPECIFIC results you want to create, remembering that each needs to be a SMART result; and THIRD and perhaps most important of all, you need to actually schedule the times to make the results happen.

Do you see the power in this? When you actually work each of these steps and schedule things in, it takes all of the mystery out of the week. Haven't you had those times when chaos sets in and you sit at your desk and you have NO idea what to do next? Well, the first place you can look now is at your calendar where, when things were calm and you were clear about what you wanted to create in this week, you wrote it down and scheduled it. You get to use your time to achieve your most cherished goals and dreams; and it's much easier to say no to the rest with this degree of clarity.

Let's move on now to daily planning. This is considerably easier once you've done your weekly planning.

You want to do this daily planning at the end of the day in anticipation of the next; or at the very start of the new day. You'll find the template on page 69.

The first thing you're going to do is look back at the experiences and the results you said you wanted to create… you're going to review your weekly plan… to get connected with it… to actually remember it in the fray of the week.

The next thing you're going to do is to adjust your scheduling to accommodate things that have arisen unexpectedly; to accommodate emergencies. Remember, though, if you've done your planning well, the likelihood of emergencies diminishes greatly.

Now, in your review, and accommodation, you're not just going to allow things to fall off your calendar. If your child gets sick in school and you can't make the yoga class, you RESCHEDULE the yoga class – just like a real appointment, a real commitment. Because this IS a real appointment, a real commitment. It's a commitment to you. You are the master of your time.

This level of detailed planning may be quite new for you. It might feel uncomfortable or forced. But any new practice or discipline does.

Commit to this weekly planning and daily planning religiously; do it every week and every day for the next 90 days. What is true is that it takes that long to dial in and hardwire any new habit. (While it sounds sexy and easy to believe that it takes just 21 days, as in a 21-day challenge, to make something automatic, scientific research demonstrates that it actually takes at least 66 days!) So just stay at it. It will transform your life. Without question; without fail. Trust the system.

Chapter 10
Go Long

I began the planning practice chapter at the weekly level and the daily level because that's the easiest and fastest point of entry. But remember, time masters play with the long view in mind. Time masters consider the grand vision for their lives; their purpose; their mission. As a time master, you'll want to do this too.

So during one of these weekend planning sessions, after you begin to get the hang of the practice, carve out a bit of extra time. Consider the grand landscape of your life.

- What is your purpose?
- What is your vision?
- What is your mission?
- What do you want to accomplish over the course of your lifetime?
- What do you want your legacy to be?

Write these things down. When we move things out of the realm of ideas and put them down on paper, they become real. Make them real.

If you were to have five goals for your lifetime, five major achievements, what would they be? Write them down.

In the back of this book, you'll find a yearly planning template on page 71; and a template for a mid-year review on page 82. They're designed particularly for use at the beginning of each calendar year; and as a means to track your progress as the year unfolds. But you can use them any time. Every day is a new beginning.

The yearly planning template is great for getting tuned into those big plans and goals that you have for your life. You'll see that it also asks you to focus on the experiences you want to have in your life because here's the scoop: if the experience is important enough for you, if your WHY is big enough, you'll figure out the how. You are the co-creator of your life. You get to make it just the way you want it.

Once you have completed your yearly planning template, you should use it as a touchstone, returning to it throughout the course of your year to assess how you're doing; and determine what kind of progress you're making toward your destination. Use the mid-year review template as a formal process to measure how you're doing.

And remember, you *will* get off course. All of us do. A plane flying from San Francisco to Hawaii is off course most of the time. But it constantly course corrects.

Think about the GPS again in your car. If you take a wrong turn, the sultry voice says, "recalculating," and gets you back on track. The same is true when you've carefully dialed in your own life plan, when you've planned your weeks and your days with care. There will be moments of uncertainty, twists and turns on the route, traffic and unexpected detours. But, with your yearly planning template, you'll always be able to "recalculate" and find your way back to your route.

One final note on this planning stuff. Some of our clients resist the process saying that it takes away spontaneity. I'm all for spontaneity. And I love free time. Plan it! Block out the time. Put the date night on the calendar, the time in the garden, the writing, painting or drawing time; the time to walk on the beach; the time to read, reflect and recollect. The challenge with our busy lives is that we like to believe that we'll make the time for these things we want to do... that when our heart's desire calls, we'll answer. The reality is that it rarely ever happens. And we look back over the course of a week... or a year... and see that the time has passed us by... again.

Time masters carve out the time for what matters most.

Chapter 11
Lights, Camera...

Yes, it's time for action.

So many folks "spend" their time thinking about acting, getting ready to act, preparing to act, planning to act, moving around the deck chairs in anticipation of whenever it might be the right time to act.

Literally this is where the rubber meets the road.

Go back to our car and GPS metaphor again. You've got the map, you've made your plan, you've locked in your destination, you're sitting in your late model Beemer and... if you don't put the key in the ignition and actually start, you will get... nowhere.

You're "wasting" time.

You must act.

One of my fondest memories from my early years as a young single dad is of watching my boy, clad in his yellow slicker and red rubber boots, stomping in the puddles, standing in the rain. He always liked being out in the "mess" of it all. Still does, I dare say.

Being out in the mess, of course, is where the action is; where it's all happening; where our lives unfold.

Not in the house; not where it's warm; not where it's dry and safe.

Out there. Out on the field.

Out where it's rough and tumble and muddy.

Out where it's cold and wet... Out where we might get hurt.

It's always interesting when coaching clients come to me with things *they say* they want to do: projects *they say* they want to pursue; goals *they say* they want to achieve; and these "things" *they say* they want to do have lived in their heads, in their minds and in their hearts... often for years... decades sometimes... as thoughts... as hopes ... as ideas... as wishes.

Of course, all great things start in our minds and hearts. There wouldn't be an electric light bulb or Sistine Chapel or car or democracy or computer or iPhone™ were it not for an idea that once lived only in someone's consciousness.

The tricky part is that next step.

The tricky part is getting out there and doing something.

The tricky part is: Taking Action.

There's a reason that comfort zones are called that.... They're pretty damn comfy. Not much is at risk. It's easy imagining a new relationship or a fresh career. It's fun to think about being a published author or an award-winning photographer. The idea of an advanced degree or a successful business is alluring... and exciting.

Doing the work: That's messy.

And overwhelming.

We fear discomfort. We fear failure. We fear criticism. We fear judgment.

We fear change.

We fear success.

And our fears keep us small. They keep us "safe" in the warm, comfy, cozy house that is our mind.

As long as we *entertain ourselves* with the ideas, as long as we *pretend* that we're going to get to it... someday... as long as we delude ourselves that, when the time is right, when the "conditions" are right, then we can somehow fool ourselves into believing that we're actually doing something.

Except that we're not.

And time goes by... and one year dissolves into the next. And the delusion stays just that.

Here's the truth: It's NEVER the right time to act. Conditions will NEVER be ideal. The time will NEVER be right.

There will ALWAYS be reasons not to pursue your hopes and dreams and aspirations.

And the clock *WILL* run out.

The time to act is now. Masters of time act NOW.

To overcome overwhelm, to combat fear: Take tiny steps. Really tiny steps. If you want to lose weight, work at losing one pound a week. If you want to start a running program, run around the block. If you want to explore a new career, take a one-week workshop. If you want a new degree, take a course, just one course. If you want to write a book, write a page (or half a page) a day.

A pound a week is 50 pounds in twelve months time. A page a day is a pretty hefty book in a year.

And how fast a year flies by.

Consistency is key. Staying at it… every day… no matter what. Braving the cold, the wet, the fear, the judgment, the discomfort.

Get it out of your head and into your life.

Make it real.

Act. Now.

Many people die with their music still in them. Why is this so? Too often it is because they are always getting ready to live. Before they know it, time runs out.

Oliver Wendell Holmes

Chapter 12
Just One Thing

We live in a culture of distraction, in a state of constant partial attention.

Alerts and alarms and banners and notifications.

We endeavor to do everything at once, never really capable of doing one thing well.

It's not a good use of time. It's not time mastery.

Did you know that every time you're distracted, every time you move from one task to another, whether it be from an email to a phone call or from a conversation to writing a note, it "costs" you 12 minutes? It takes the brain 12 minutes to settle down to the new task and become completely focused... until it's distracted again.

So let's apply a bit of math, shall we? Let's say that, this morning, you're "distracted" ten times. Ten distractions times 12 minutes per distraction equals a loss of two hours of time. I bet that the number of distractions that you entertain in a day far exceeds ten.

If you're reading this book, you likely pride yourself on your ability to multi-task, right? I know I do! I think I'm damn good at it!

But multi-tasking is a myth. We can't do it. It can't be done! Physiologically it can't be done. Our brains aren't wired that way. Our brains work sequentially. One thing and then the next thing.

Now some of us have gotten quite adept at working sequentially. And we can do it pretty damn fast. So fast, in fact, that we think we're actually doing it all at once. But what we're really doing is toggling back and forth, back and forth, and back and forth...you get my drift... until utter exhaustion sets in.

Masters focus on just one thing at a time. One conversation, one project, one email. And when we bring our whole attention to just the one thing, we're able to attend to it wholly, completely and fully.

Think about that last conversation you had with your team member… or your child. What was going on in your life? In your brain? Where you reading the email while you were "listening?" Were you thinking about what you needed to do next while you were "speaking?"

Think about that last networking event you went to. You're having a conversation with someone new. And then you see it. The gaze broken just for the fraction of an instant, the momentary glance just over your shoulder. And you know the conversation is over… time to move on… to someone, something "more" important.

What if *this* was most important? This thing, this conversation, this person, this moment? The most important thing in the entire world. This. Here. Now.

How would that change the dynamic? How would that change your focus? How would that impact your efficiency?

How much more engaged you would be. How much more honor you would bring to your partners, your team, your staff, your work, your life.

Do just one thing at a time. That's what masters do.

Try working in "block time."

Our daylight hours are much like our sleep time. We're awake in pulses and rhythms of attention. We work best in 60 to 90 minute blocks.

If you have a Power Point™ you need to finish, shut your door; turn off your alerts; close all your browser windows; turn off your phone. Work on just your Power Point™ for 60 to 90 minutes. Nothing else. Just that.

When you're done, take a break. Walk down to the water cooler, step outside for some fresh air, listen to some music for a few minutes, read a chapter from your book, breath, relax, just be.

And then get back to the project, to the Power Point™, or to a new project. Another 60 to 90 minutes. Uninterrupted, undistracted.

Choose blocks of time for your phone calls, for your emails, for your team meetings. Choose blocks for your social media engagement. Choose designated times for checking your smartphone. (Some studies show that people check their smartphones as often as 900 times a day.

Try doing that math for the "cost" of distraction!)

Yes, I know that you've got a lot to do. And people "expect" that you'll be at their beck and call. I get that. I spent decades as a trial lawyer. I get that everything is an emergency. Except not much really is.

We lead by example. We train people how to treat us. Train others well. Because how you treat yourself ultimately is how you'll treat those around you. Honor yourself. Honor those with whom you serve in each and every moment.

Ask your assistant to hold your calls when you're meeting with an employee or a team member. Set an auto-responder for your emails telling folks that you check your emails two or three times a day at designated times (blocks).

Create smartphone free zones and meetings; don't put your smartphone on the dinner table. Don't bring it into the bedroom.

Be with what you're doing; and just what you're doing. Nothing else. Your effectiveness will skyrocket. Your resiliency will soar. Your care and attention too.

Chapter 13
The Meeting Maze

The Maze was a movie about a group of boys locked in a futuristic experiment. To escape their stockade-like confines, they needed to navigate a complicated maze filled with life-threatening dangers.

Meetings are like that.

Sometimes I think that the world will end in a gridlocked meeting. Meetings can be dire. And they will suck your time away.

Masters of time are wary of meetings. They'll meet; but only as a last resort.

If you are in a leadership role (*i.e.* you are the scheduler of meetings), ask yourself whether a meeting is essential to your goals before setting up a meeting; consider whether you can achieve your objectives without a meeting. Don't just default to setting up a meeting because that's what's always been done. (Many organizations have a culture of meetings. These are often the organizations that hire me to train their teams in time mastery!)

Consider too whether live and in-person meetings are essential to your outcomes, or whether you can accomplish your goals by way of teleconference or a platform such as GoToMeeting™. Dragging people out of their offices, across town or from around the country can be a huge time sink in and of itself, putting aside the ancillary time and expense.

Now, if you're a team member, listen carefully. All meetings are not created equal. Some are essential (as in they are a requirement of your job). Others, though, *may not* be required. Don't assume that every invitation for a meeting must be accepted; don't go to every meeting if you don't have to. If in doubt, ask your supervisor. When done respectfully and with an eye on your end result, he or she will honor you for seeking to be a wise steward of your time.

Ok, so you've decided to have (or go to) a meeting.

In order for meetings to be productive, there must be a clear, concise, specific, written agenda.

There must be a defined purpose and outcome for the meeting. That is, a meeting for the sake of meeting is nothing other than a maze.

Meeting must be time-defined; open-ended meetings are recipes for marathon disasters.

Meetings must start on time; and they must end on time. There is no waiting for latecomers.

Unless technology assists, such as laptops or tablets, are specifically required to fulfill the agenda, meetings should be tech-free. Cell phones should be turned OFF.

There shall not be death by PowerPoint™. You know what I mean by this: Endless slides densely packed with text that is then read by the presenter.

A strong leader must preside over a meeting. By strong, I mean a leader who is able to keep the meeting participants focused on the specified purpose and the outcome of the meeting, following the written agenda, within the time period prescribed. A strong leader empowers each attendee to participate, eliciting input and points of view, but carefully controls the agenda, and unabashedly cuts off unfocused ramblers and efforts to deviate.

The highest and best value of a meeting is about relationship, about connection; about being with others who share your mission; exchanging ideas; collaborating; working toward a common goal. It's about creativity. It's about the opportunity to affirm, inspire and empower.

If your meeting doesn't contain these ingredients, think hard before you get lost in the maze.

Chapter 14
The Monster Lurking Within

There's a wonderful children's book entitled *The Monster Under My Bed* by James Howe. I can't count the number of times I read it to my kids to assuage their fears of the dark.

As they – and all of us – eventually discovered, there was no monster under the bed. But there is one waiting for you. It's called your email Inbox.

At every Time Mastery workshop I do, one of the very first questions I get asked is about how to tame this monster. How do I get control of my Inbox?

One CEO admitted to me that he had 2000 unanswered emails in his Inbox. Another shared that he had over 30,000 emails in his Inbox… unfiled.

Email dogs us incessantly. Every time we go in to answer one, a dozen others pop up. A virtual Hydra. Add to that the tones and pings that alert us to a new message, and we have a time mastery nightmare on our hands.

So I want to share with you some principles that will allow you to wrestle this monster to the ground once and for all.

First, don't check your email first thing in the morning. I am dead serious about this. If you have gotten clear on what you value most (Chapter 2) and you have a defined Plan (Chapter 7), and you set out to achieve specific goals (Chapter 8), and you've dialed in solid practices (Chapter 9), then your email Inbox is someone else's agenda for your day! Once you've checked your Inbox, you've been hijacked… if not actually by feeling compelled to respond in that very moment, then at least energetically by virtue of thinking (or ruminating) on what your response will be.

I've made that mistake from time to time before going out on my morning run. My run is one of my most creative and resourceful times of the day. And rather than reveling in the moment, allowing my mind to clear and focus on my most cherished projects, the email message rattles around in my head, sucking the energy right out of me.

Your email Inbox can wait until you've taken care of your own high-value targets.

Second, set aside blocks of time in the day (remember Chapter 12) dedicated to checking and responding to emails. Don't do it all day long every time you hear an alert. In fact, turn off the alerts! There's a cost to distraction, and it's *huge* as you'll discover in the next chapter. Schedule two or three blocks, say 9:00 to 9:30 in the morning; 12:30 to 1:00 pm midday; and 4:30 to 5:00 at the end of the day.

If you're really paranoid that you'll miss something important, use an auto-responder, perhaps something like this: *I check and respond to my emails three times at day at 9:00 a.m., noon, and again at 4:00 p.m. If you have an urgent matter, please call my assistant at 555-555-5555.*

No disaster will befall you if you don't constantly check your email. I once went away on a month-long climbing expedition and came back to an Inbox of nearly 3000 emails. There were no insurmountable challenges. Prior to departing, my Irish Catholic mother had worried that someone might die in my absence and I wouldn't know about it. I assured her that that person would still be dead when I returned.

So you've attended to your high-value targets and you're ready to tackle the monster. What do you do now?

Apply the 3 Ds: Do, Delegate or Delete.

By Do, I mean respond in that moment to the email; or if it requires no response and is important as a record, file it in an appropriate folder, moving from your Inbox.

Delegate means forwarding it, in that moment, to your assistant or colleague together with appropriate instructions to be handled by that other person.

Delete means getting rid of it. Right then.

By the way, take the time, in the first instance, to unsubscribe to unwanted emails or mark them as spam (of course, the exception to this would be emails from me). And set appropriate filters to segregate emails for easier review. (Gmail is especially useful for this practice.)

Ok, you say… but I'm the CEO with 2000 unanswered emails in my Inbox. I'm drowning. Tell me where to start.

Declare email amnesty. Set up a file folder called Old Inbox. Move your entire Inbox to that folder. And start again.

This way, you can begin anew with these more powerful practices. If something crops up from an old email, you'll be able to find it. The likelihood is that you'll discover that the Old Inbox is kinda like that shabby cardboard box that's been sitting in the back of your garage for the last 6 years… good for not much of anything. But, of course, if you're in a profession like law or medicine or financial services, you probably shouldn't chuck it.

When I was a student at Cornell Law School, there was a grand old movie about legal education called *The Paper Chase.* Indeed, when I first started practice, it was all about the paper. Email and its attendant technologies was supposed to cure us of that. But alas, we've been left with a monster.

But it *can* be tamed.

Chapter 15
Check Your Sinks

No, this is not a chapter on plumbing or bathroom fixtures. But all of us have places where we "lose" time.

Time sinks.

At nearly every book signing I do, someone will say to me, "Wow, I'd love to write a book. I wish I had the time."

You do.

You can write a novel, start a new business, launch a new product, volunteer at a nursing home, start a fitness program, take up ballroom dance or learn to scuba dive. In fact, you might be able do them all.

You have the time. It's just that so much of it gets squandered.

The average amount of time that folks watch television is 34 hours a week. That's, like, nearly a full-time job.

Folks spend more than 22 hours a week on social media.

Add just those two numbers together and you're up to 52 hours a week in time you might use in other endeavors! That's more than two full days!

What could you do with two extra days a week?

Then there's the "cost" of distraction.

Our cultural insistence on multitasking (which, as we discussed earlier, simply can't be done) reduces our productivity by as much as 40%! And not only that, but it also drops our IQ by as much a 15 points. (Do you really want to negotiate an important deal or land your next client in a state like that?)

Further, studies show that once we get distracted from a task we're working on, whether by a phone call or email or conversation, it actually takes between 12 and 25 minutes to get back on task. If you're distracted just 10 times in a day (and I know that it's way more than that), the time "lost" is 250 minutes… over 4 hours in a day!

The average number of times people check their smartphones is 150 times a day. One recent study found folks checking their phones as many as 900 times in a day. But let's go with the lower number and multiply it by a more conservative "cost" of distraction, say 12 minutes. The result is a "lost" 30 hours in a day. Talk about deficit spending!

You might want to try a "time inventory," much like you'd do a spending inventory with your money. For a week, track how you're spending your time. Keep a running tally. Write it down. Then you can assess how you might want to re-allocate it.

All of us need down time. We'll talk about that in a bit. It's ok to surf the net or watch the tube. But don't default to the excuse that you don't have the time for what you really want. Because I'm betting that you do. Simply becoming more mindful of how you're spending your time will open up vast reservoirs that you didn't know existed.

And then, world, watch out. What you will be able create in that time will be astounding!

Chapter 16
Are You All In?

Clarity is the key, we tell our coaching clients. You can't hit a target you can't see.

Action too is essential. Without action, you get nowhere.

But while these principles are true, they're not the whole story. You can be clear as a bell; you can take any number of steps toward your goal; and still not get the outcome you seek.

The goal will elude you.

Unless you're "all in."

I remember as a young associate at a big law firm being quite clear that I wanted my own business, my own practice. I can remember thinking about it (for a *long* time), talking with colleagues about it, buying books about it, reading about it, researching what it would take, even ordering business cards! But until I actually put the date on the calendar on which I was going to quit the big firm, until I announced to the partners that I was leaving, until I tendered my written resignation, it all stayed safely within the realm of fantasy.

I hadn't been all in.

On a recent coaching call, a client shared with me his frustration over the lack of progress in his business development. Growth was flat, he said. Turns out he was continuing to work on other projects... giving only intermittent attention to his real goal, his real love; still tentative... because he wasn't yet... all in.

There was still uncertainty; still ambiguity and ambivalence. Still the possibility of turning back. And it was showing up - unambiguously - in the bottom line.

My wife, Ann, and I have the best gig on the planet. We so value the depth of the relationship we share... and the fun... What's interesting though is that our relationship grew exponentially strong *after* we were married... when we finally knew in the depths of our hearts that we were all in.

There's that ancient military adage: If you want to take the island, burn the boats.

In business, finance, careers, start-ups, product launches, creative endeavors, relationships, fitness; whatever the goal... if it's important enough: Commit.

Go all in.

Allow no means of escape.

I'm not suggesting this is easy. In fact it's downright scary. And sometimes it needs to be a process... not a moment... and that's ok.

But here's what's true: when you're all in, the magic happens.

As acclaimed Scottish mountaineer W. H. Murray wrote,

> Until one is committed, there is hesitancy, the chance to draw back, always ineffectiveness. Concerning all acts of initiative (and creation), there is one elementary truth the ignorance of which kills countless ideas and splendid plans: that the moment one definitely commits oneself, then providence moves too. A whole stream of events issues from the decision, raising in one's favor all manner of unforeseen incidents, meetings and material assistance, which no man could have dreamt would have come his way. I learned a deep respect for one of Goethe's couplets: Whatever you can do or dream you can, begin it. Boldness has genius, power and magic in it!

So if there's an area of your life that's not quite clicking, ask yourself, "Have I burned the boats? Am I all in?"

Chapter 17
In The Mood

The bed was warm. She cozied closer.

"Are you in the mood?" Ann asked.

I looked at her, my eyes wide in disbelief.

"What are you, on crack?" I asked. "Of course, I'm NOT in the mood."

Who asks questions like that? It was cold outside, 18 degrees as I recall. And dark. Who wants to run in the cold and dark?

She was joking, of course. It's not a question we ask… or entertain about our running. At least not often.

Because, for pursuits of any import, mood is irrelevant.

I'm rarely in the mood to go to the gym. I'm never in the mood to count my calories or sort my supplements. I'm only occasionally in the mood to run. Sometimes I'm in the mood to write. And sometimes not. I love to photograph. But I'm never in the mood to edit. I'm passionate about speaking. But the preparation is tedious.

Rory Vaden writes, "Simply stated, there are only two types of activities: things we feel like doing and things we don't. And if we can learn to make ourselves do the things we don't want to do, then we have literally created the power to create any result in our lives."

Successful people do whatever they need to do to achieve their goals, regardless of how they "feel."

"Successful people are successful because they form the habits of doing those things that failures don't like to do," said Albert Gray.

Form the habits of success. Dial in the gym, the run, the weekly planning, the healthy meals. Schedule and commit the time to write, to paint, to practice the instrument. Do what's really important. Do it every day. Don't think about it. Don't analyze it. Don't wonder about it. Don't worry about it. Don't re-consider it. Do it. Just do it. No matter what.

When was the last time you asked yourself whether you were "in the mood" to brush your teeth? What a ridiculous question to ask, you say. Make your habits of success like that.

The things that look effortless, the performances that are flawless, the achievements that astound (all those things you're jealous of): they're borne of countless hours of practice and preparation. Of doing. And doing again. And had nothing to do with mood.

So if the new business venture is on your list, or the MBA, or the 5k in the spring, now is the time to start.

I don't care if you're in the mood, or not. You are a master.

Chapter 18
Mojo

I had just finished speaking to a university audience on leadership and goal achievement, and had stayed on afterwards to chat with the students.

"I know *exactly* what I want," my young listener proclaimed.

Looking earnest, he furled his brow. "It's just that I don't always *feel* very motivated."

"I don't really give a damn what you feel," I replied with an equal amount of furling and earnestness.

"If you know *exactly* what you want… and you want it badly enough, then you'll show up every day and do what needs to be done *whether you feel like it or not.*"

He flinched, only slightly, as I jabbed my finger in the air for extra dramatic import: "Motivation is vastly overrated."

And it is.

I love to ice climb but I rarely feel motivated to put on my heavy mitts to go out into the arctic cold to do it. There's not a whole lot of motivation going on when I think about driving three hours to a ski area or hoisting the kayaks onto the roof of a car. I almost never feel motivated to write. In fact, I've put off writing this chapter until the very last moment possible, perhaps just to dramatically punctuate my own perpetual lack of motivation!

You see, motivation just like mood, is flighty. It's not dependable. It comes… and it goes. Sometimes it shows up; more often than not, it doesn't. Even when it comes to stuff we like or want.

What's important is the *knowing*. Knowing what you want. Knowing what you like. Knowing where it is you want to go. *And why.*

When you're clear about your destination, when you know your outcome, then all you need to do is act. You're pulled forward by the vision of what you'll achieve. Whether you feel motivated from moment to moment is irrelevant. In fact, your transitory perceptions about whether you're motivated or not usually just end up getting in the way.

I know how much I value my fitness and vitality over time when I run. And so I run. Whether I'm motivated or not.

I know how much I love the creative process of writing and the sense of satisfaction I have when the words I've written have an impact on someone I've never even met. So I write.

Whether I'm motivated or not.

Get clear on what *you* really, *really* want.

Then get going. And stay at it.

In the meantime, it doesn't really much matter how motivated you are. Because with clarity and conviction, you become a master of your time. And you will accomplish your most cherished goals.

Chapter 19
Staying At it

Financial objectives; weight loss; fitness goals; career ladders; creative projects: sometimes it feels as if we're making no forward progress; sometimes it feels as if we're sliding backwards; in fact, sometimes it seems as if we're caught in a deep dark hole.

If the goal is worthy and the strategy sound, there's only one real course of action: keep on keepin' on.

I remember years ago, right after they re-opened Mt. St. Helens, my son, Joe, and I climbed to the crater rim. Seismically unstable, the trail had been shut down for years; the landscape scorched and shattered.

As we emerged from the forest, the upper slopes were covered with ash. We'd take a step up, and slide back; another step up, another slide back. It was like hiking on a beach that had been pitched at a 45° angle, grinding and relentless.

In the clear air under the hot sun, we could see our objective. But it never seemed to get any closer. Morale flagged; we were tempted to give up; it was so discouraging.

And so it often is.

When we get bogged down, it's easy to get despondent, to lose the focus and resolve. We feel like quitting. But here's the truth: it's the small, steady efforts that yield the rewards. Over time, the plodding matters.

We hung our feet over the crater rim and laughed. The seeming futility throughout the effort of the climb had been almost comic. Yet the reward of that spectacular moment was beyond compare.

Darren Hardy, the publisher of Success Magazine, tells the story of the man who cut his calorie consumption by just 125 calories a day;

less than the "price" of a cup of cereal. After 31 months, the man had lost 33 ½ pounds. (125 calories a day x 940 days=117,500 calories x 1 pound/3500 calories=33 ½ pounds). I wonder how many times this dude looked in the mirror and said, "damn, I still look fat."

At mile 32 of the Vermont 50 miler, I sat and wept. Thirty-two miles was the farthest I'd ever run before; and 18 miles more seemed incomprehensible to me. I stood up and plodded onward: I picked those 18 off just one mile at a time.

I love the story of Cliff Young. It's a story of audaciousness... but even more than that, it's a study in tenacity... stick-to-it-ness... something that all of us can use sometimes...

Cliff Young was a 61-year-old potato farmer who had never run a race before. He decided he wanted to run the Sydney to Melbourne, Australia Ultra Marathon... 543.7 miles! He arrived at the starting line wearing overalls and gumboots. The race officials wanted to deny him entry to the race fearing that he would collapse and die. Bad for publicity, they thought.

Cliff argued that he really did have experience. He told the officials and the press that he had previously run for two to three days straight rounding up sheep.

The race officials eventually relented. At a loping pace, Cliff ran continually for 5 days, 15 hours, beating all five of his competitors. He won. And not only did he win, but he beat the course record by two days!!! Because he didn't know he was supposed to stop and eat and sleep.

He just kept going.

Keep going. That's the lesson. That's the secret that time masters know.

In our lives, it's one resume at a time in the job search; a few dollars more building our empire; an extra crunch or two that gets us fit; just another chapter toward the completion of that book. It's one more draft; another rejection; another practice session; a couple more laps around the track; just a lesson or two more.

Once we're clear about where we want to go, just keep going. One step at a time.

Ever tried. Ever Failed. No Matter. Try again. Fail again. Fail better.
Samuel Beckett

Chapter 20
Re-Create

This power principle isn't found in many time management books. But it is essential.

We – all of us – need down time, time away from our work, time off the grid, time away.

We're not built like machines. We can't run 24/7/365. It's not sustainable. And yet, we pretend that we can; that we can keep on going, no matter what; that we don't need days off; that vacations are for sissies.

When I first started at the "Big Firm," the mentor giving me my "orientation" told me, "You get three weeks of vacation; and you can't take them all at once." Then he dropped his voice an octave and looked at me sternly saying, "And of course, no one ever takes them."

I promptly booked three weeks vacation.

Vacations are essential for our well-being. Without vacations, our focus decays, our efficiency erodes, and our productivity drops. It takes longer to accomplish tasks that we could do faster if we were fresher. We're more prone to mistakes.

Without vacations, fatigue increases, stress increases, we become more susceptible to illness and our risk for heart disease soars.

Without vacations, we become sloppy and inefficient with our time.

The average U.S. worker uses only half of their paid time off. Last year there were 577,212,000 vacation days left on the table. This is poor time allocation. Not mastery.

By the way, I usually take about 12 weeks of vacation every year. But if you've got days you don't want, I'll take them.

In a similar manner, periodic days off are essential to our mastery of time. They renew and refresh us. We re-charge and refocus. We come back stronger, more resilient and more productive.

Even during a day, it's essential to step away from what we're doing. As I mentioned in Chapter 12, physiologically and neurologically, we don't work in a linear fashion. Our energy and attention rises and falls throughout the day. And it's important to honor and engage those natural rhythms.

Experiment. Become aware of your own rhythms. Work in time blocks of 60 to 90 minutes. Take breaks in between. Go for a walk, listen to some music, enjoy some quiet or read. You'll come back to your work with much more efficiency. Your use of time will skyrocket.

By the way, there's another little "vacation" concept that you get to use every day... and probably don't do very well. It's called sleep.

If you use this practice to your advantage, you can actually sleep your way to the top, as Arianna Huffington quips!

Research clearly shows that we need 7 to 9 hours of sleep every single night. (To find out how much you need, experiment with not setting an alarm. Your body will actually tell you!) And a lot of us – half the population - don't get nearly enough.

I used to pride myself on being able to "function" on 5 or 6 hours of sleep a night. What that's called is functional delusion.

Entrepreneurs, accountants, lawyers, doctors, and countless other professionals think that it's "normal" not to sleep for days or weeks on end.

Sleep deprivation significantly erodes focus and attention, dramatically reduces short and long term memory, impedes planning, prejudices decision making and judgment, compromises your immune system, and spikes your risk for heart disease and cardiac arrest.

You're not using time very well.

The Chernobyl disaster, Three Mile Island, the Challenger explosion, the wreck of the Exxon Valdez, and numerous train and airline crashes have all been related in one way or another to sleep deprivation.

Is your work, your family, your life really worth these risks?

Moreover, wouldn't you prefer to enjoy laser focus, high engagement, and turbo-charged energy?

You can. If you get enough sleep.

And when you're awake, you need to feed and fuel and care for yourself if you're going to be masters of your time.

We teach our coaching clients the Health Triad, the three Es: the elements of Eating, Exercise and Emotional Wellbeing. I'm not going to turn this into a health and wellness book. But while it may be cliché to say that without your health, you have nothing, it's also axiomatic. And yet so many of us go about our days as if our health is just a given... or as if our health would be something nice to attend to someday... as in it would be nice someday to clean out the garage.

The reality is that there are a lot of rich, successful folks who can't enjoy a damn thing... because they let their health go... and they can't get it back... because it's too late.

Health and wellness are NOT secondary considerations. They are core principles of success. In fact, they are THE CORE principles of success.

We give a lot of attention to business building, research, product launches, marketing, client development, and wealth accumulation. Would that we might give the same attention to our health.

Despite the multi-million dollar industry that surrounds the eating stuff, it's not terribly complicated. Don't eat **CRAP** (**C**arbonated stuff, **R**efined sugars, **A**rtificial sweeteners and colors, or **P**rocessed foods). Eat more **FOOD** (**F**resh fruits and vegetables, **O**rganic lean protein, **O**mega 3 fatty acids, and **D**rink plenty of water). Exercise is about MOVING your body. And emotional wellbeing is about reconnecting with your own ground, perhaps through a simple mediation practice, opening up more time, and creating more space.

Finally, if you're going to be a true time master, you need to use the f** word often. Fun.

Too many of us have forgotten fun. And fun is essential to our success.

Stuart Brown, a psychiatrist and founder of the National Institute for Play in California, says active play is necessary to build our brains into "responsive, flexible, skilled and more social instruments." Good stuff if we're going to excel in our work; and necessary if we're going to be good stewards of our time.

So this whole re-create thing is another paradox... flying directly in the face of what we've been inculcated with culturally; contravening many of our own puritanical natures; and often at odds with corporate culture. Yet, without re-creating, (yes, you can read this recreating), we become sloppy and inefficient with our time, we lose our focus, attention and productivity; and we put ourselves and others at serious risk.

Chapter 21
Culture Wars

I'm a Boomer. So I can Boomer bash.

When I first started at the Big Firm, we were expected to bill 1800 hours a year. By the time I left, that number had risen to 2200 hours. It was (and is) unsustainable.

Time is money they said.

"Face time" was exalted... it was important, we were told, for the partners to "see" us in the office late at night, early in the morning, on weekends and holidays... sometimes it seemed that being "seen" was even more important than the quality of work we turned out.

Vacations were eschewed. Vacations were for sissies. Didn't matter whether you were sick or tired or both. Didn't matter what else was going on in your life. Just didn't matter.

But it matters.

Happily corporate cultures are beginning to change. The quality of the work product has begun to supplant face time. Flextime and telecommuting are no longer oddities.

There is a much higher awareness of sustainability; a much greater respect for health, emotional wellness and mindfulness; and a much higher regard for what happens beyond the hallowed corporate halls.

But the change has been slow... and Boomers have dragged their heels.

I get asked regularly at workshops by young women and men starting out in their careers about how to adopt many of the principles I teach in this book, especially if their bosses don't "get it" and don't approve. It's a tough spot to be in. And there isn't an easy answer.

Leadership comes from above; but also from below. I believe that all of us are leaders regardless of title or position. All of us are responsible for teaching and advocating principles that will enrich the corporate culture and support our mission in the world.

The answer is to communicate clearly, to create meaningful dialogue, to challenge the *status quo*, and have the courage to experiment with new practices that can improve and enhance the lives of all.

Changing and improving corporate culture takes time... it takes persistence. And even older Boomers can be taught new tricks.

Chapter 22
In The End

At the end of our lives, it won't matter how many hours you billed, how many clients you saw, how many units you sold. It won't matter how many LinkedIn connections you have, how often you've updated your status on Facebook, or how often you tweeted your pithy words of wisdom.

What will matter will be the experiences you've had, the lives you've touched, the wisdom you've passed on, the love that you've shared.

What will matter is whether you've lived without regret.

Steve Jobs once said, "For the past 33 years, I have looked in the mirror every morning and asked myself: 'If today were the last day of my life, would I want to do what I am about to do today?' And whenever the answer has been 'No' for too many days in a row, I know I need to change something."

He also wrote, "Your time is limited, so don't waste it living someone else's life. Don't be trapped by dogma - which is living with the results of other people's thinking. Don't let the noise of other's opinions drown out your own inner voice. And most important, have the courage to follow your heart and intuition. They somehow already know what you truly want to become. Everything else is secondary."

Jobs knew the importance of time. Masters do.

Some scientists believe that time is linear. More recently, physicists have hypothesized that time is all laid out on a landscape palette, past, present and future, all before us. I think time is more like the wind. We can feel it blow across our face. We can see it in the mirror and in the faded photos in our drawer. We can perceive its impact on the lives around us and upon the world we live in.

But we can never grab hold of it, we can never bottle it. We can never wrestle it to the ground. And we certainly can never "manage" it.

We can, though, become masters. Masters of our time; masters of our destiny. And we can leave the world a better place for having been here.

So long as we remember: There is no time.

Your inbox will still be full when you die. There will be phone calls to return and closets to clean. But no matter.

Life is not about ticking off a list; it's not about the toys or the corner office.

And, as Hunter Thompson said, "Life is not a journey to the grave with the intention of arriving safely in a well preserved body, but rather to skid in broadside, thoroughly used up, totally worn out, and loudly proclaiming, "Wow what a ride!"

May you become a master of this wondrous ride.

Appendix

Values Exercise

What I Value: How I Spend Time:

1. _____   1._____

2. _____   2._____

3. _____   3._____

4. _____   4._____

5. _____   5._____

My Stop Doing List:

1. _____

2. _____

3. _____

4. _____

5. _____

6. _____

7. _____

8. _____

9. _____

10. _____

Weekly Planning Template

Week of: _____

Set aside a block of time on the weekend, an hour or so, to plan your next week. Thinking about the different areas of your life, what specific *experiences* and *results* do you want to create in the week ahead?

Financial:

Career/Business:

Health/Wellness/Appearance:

Personal:

Free time/Family Time:

Relationships:

Community:

Do those experiences and results that you want to create translate into specific, concrete activities that you need to schedule? What are they and *when* will you do them?

➤

➤

➤

➤

➤

➤

➤

➤

➤

➤

➤

➤

Notes:

Now here's the key: Right now, commit and schedule. Get out your planner, your day timer, your Outlook, your gCal, and actually block out the time that you are going to do these activities.

Have a great week. Make it a masterpiece!

Daily Planning Template

Date: _____

Review your weekly plan. What are the specific *experiences* and *results* that you set as your intentions this week?

What are the *experiences* that you would like to have *today*?

What are the *concrete results* that you would like to create *today*?

What are your **3 Most Important Things** today? (Your MITs)

1.

2.

3.

Review your calendar or day timer. Are your MITs *scheduled* in? What additions/deletions to you need to make to your schedule?

Note any necessary adjustments to your scheduling. Remember the 80/20 rule!

And then, make it an awesome day.

Yearly Planning

This Past Year

What were my successes this year? What did I accomplish? What went especially well? What am I proud of having completed?

1. _____

2. _____

3. _____

4. _____

5. _____

How did I celebrate my successes this year?

1. _____

2. _____

3. _____

4. _____

5. _____

What were my "magic moments" this year? What great memories do I have? What special times and memories did I create for others?

1. _____

2. _____

3. _____

4. _____

5. _____

What specific goals and/or resolutions did I set for myself this past year and which ones did I accomplish?

1. _____[ ] Y [ ] N

2. _____[ ] Y [ ] N

3. _____[ ] Y [ ] N

4. _____[ ] Y [ ] N

5. _____[ ] Y [ ] N

For the goals that I achieved, what factors, practices, disciplines led to their achievement?

1. _____

2. _____

3. _____

4. _____

5. _____

For the goals that I didn't complete, what got in the way?

1. _____

2. _____

3. _____

4. _____

5. _____

What practices and disciplines would be useful to continue?

1. _____

2. _____

3. _____

4. _____

5. _____

As you sit here today, how does your "Wheel of Life" look? Rate yourself in each of the major areas of your life on a scale of 1 to 10; 1 being closest to the center and 10 being on the outside of the wheel. Draw in the lines. How is your wheel rolling?

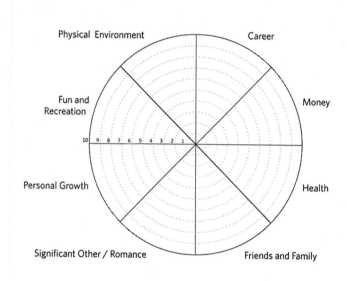

The Year Ahead:

A year from now, what would you like your "Wheel of Life" to look like? Draw in the lines; see how it will be.

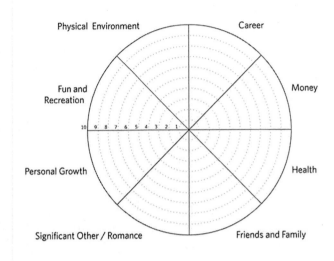

What specific goals are you going to commit to achieving during the year ahead? By what date will you achieve these goals? Why do you want to achieve these goals; what's the purpose? Why are these goals a "must" for you? BE SPECIFIC.

Goal #1

_____

_____

I will achieve this goal by: _____

Why? What's my purpose?

_____

_____

Why is this goal a "must" for me?

_____

_____

What will be the consequence of not achieving this goal?

_____

_____

What specific actions do I need to take to achieve this goal?

_____

_____

Goal #2

_____

_____

I will achieve this goal by:_____

Why? What's my purpose?

_____

_____

Why is this goal a "must" for me?

_____

_____

What will be the consequence of not achieving this goal?

_____

_____

What specific actions do I need to take to achieve this goal?

_____

_____

Goal #3

_____

_____

I will achieve this goal by:_____

Why? What's my purpose?

_____

_____

Why is this goal a "must" for me?

_____

_____

What will be the consequence of not achieving this goal?

_____

_____

What specific actions do I need to take to achieve this goal?

_____

_____

Goal #4

_____

_____

I will achieve this goal by:_____

Why? What's my purpose?

_____

_____

Why is this goal a "must" for me?

_____

_____

What will be the consequence of not achieving this goal?

_____

_____

What specific actions do I need to take to achieve this goal?

_____

_____

Goal #5

_____

_____

I will achieve this goal by:_____

Why? What's my purpose?

_____

_____

Why is this goal a "must" for me?

_____

_____

What will be the consequence of not achieving this goal?

_____

_____

What specific actions do I need to take to achieve this goal?

_____

_____

What practices and disciplines am I going to commit to in the year ahead?

1. _____

2. _____

3. _____

4. _____

5. _____

What "magic moments" do I want to create for myself and for those I love in the year ahead?

1. _____

2. _____

3. _____

4. _____

5. _____

How will I celebrate my successes in the year ahead?

1. _____

2. _____

3. _____

4. _____

5. _____

NOTES:

_____

_____

_____

_____

Mid-Year Review

What we focus on expands. So let's focus first on our 'wins.' What's gone especially well in the first half of the year? What have been your 'wins'? What have been your greatest accomplishments?

1. _____

2. _____

3. _____

4. _____

5. _____

In the same way, bringing focus to what's good in our lives leads to an even greater awareness of what's working well. What are you grateful for as you come to this halfway point in the year?

1. _____

2. _____

3. _____

4. _____

5. _____

Now, when you sat down at the beginning of this year... way back at the end of December (even if you didn't do it formally), what were your 'resolutions'? What were your hopes and dreams and aspirations for the year? What major goals did you set?

1. _____

2. _____

3. _____

4. _____

5. _____

6.

How are you doing with these goals? Which ones have you accomplished? Which ones are you putting aside (and why)? Which ones are you making good progress on? Which ones do you want to focus on now?

1. _____

2. _____

3. _____

4. _____

5. _____

What have your challenges been this year? What obstacles have you encountered? What's been getting in the way? What have been your 'sticky' points? And, most important, what are you going to do with these going forward?

_____

_____

_____

_____

_____

_____

Now looking forward, what are your goals for the next 6 months? What do you want to accomplish before the end of the year? What are your 'musts'? What has to happen to make it your best year ever?

1. _____

2. _____

3. _____

4. _____

5. _____

What disciplines and practices do you need to put in place in order to accomplish these goals? What are the specific action steps you need to take... and WHEN (exactly) are you going to take them?

1. _____

2. _____

3. _____

4. _____

5. _____

COMMIT to these disciplines, practices and action steps by actually scheduling them on your calendaring system.

How's your 'wheel of life' as you look at how things are here at half-time? Rate yourself in each of the major areas of your life:

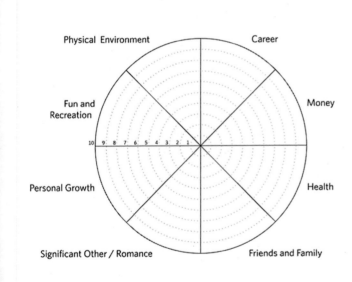

This IS the wheel you're rolling on… How would you like it to look 6 month hence? Draw it the way you want it to be:

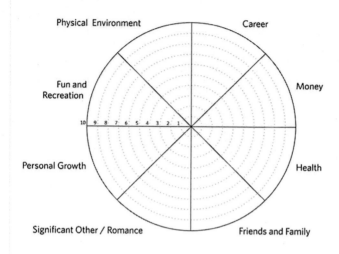

The year is either half over... or half begun. Let's go with half begun. You've reviewed your progress. You've set your intention. You've made the plan. Now let's begin again.

Acknowledgements

The power principles of time mastery are a work in process. All of us struggle with this elusive thing called time. And for all of us, there are days that we have wasted horribly and days of shining brilliance; and then there are all of those days in between during which we strive to master what we can. We teach what we most need to know.

My years as a single dad taught me humility and patience. Children are often our greatest teachers when it comes to time and what matters most. I am so grateful for the gift of my children, Maria, Joe, Zak and Luke. I cannot imagine a prouder dad than I.

My long-time coach, mentor and dear, dear friend, Tama Kieves, who wrote the magnificent Foreword to *Journeys on the Edge: Living a Life That Matters*, is a brilliant example of someone who lives in this world richly, fully, and deeply; and who constantly reminds me of how essential it is to listen to that Spirit that calls within all of us; that Spirit that transcends all time. She is the author of *two* bestsellers, *This Time I Dance! Creating the Work You Love, Inspired & Unstoppable: Wildly Succeeding in Your Life's Work!* and her new book, *A Year Without Fear: 365 Days of Magnificence.* I am so grateful for her presence in my life.

This Second Edition has been greatly enriched and enhanced by the beautiful Foreword graciously and generously scripted by the inestimable Bob Vanourek. Bob has captained the ship at five major corporations; and has to his credit an award-winning leadership book, *Triple Crown Leadership: Building Excellent, Ethical, and Enduring Organizations.* He is a true Master. I am blessed to call him a dear friend.

I am forever grateful too for my wonderful friend Maryanna Young at Aloha Publishing, the awesome house that published *Journeys.* She is a constant source of inspiration and encouragement.

And, of course, my dearest Ann, my muse, my lover, my very best friend: How very blessed am I to spend my time with you.

About Walt

Walt Hampton, J.D., is an executive coach, business consultant and leadership trainer. He is an internationally acclaimed motivational speaker and the best-selling author of *Journeys on the Edge: Living a Life That Matters*. Ivy-trained as a trial lawyer, Walt is a high altitude mountaineer, ultra-distance runner, blue-water sailor and adventure photographer.

Together with his wife, the writer Ann Sheybani, Walt lives in Collinsville, Connecticut and Castletownshend, Ireland. Between them they have six children and many dogs.

For meeting planners: To book Walt to speak, for information about his workshops and seminars, or to inquire regarding bulk purchases of this book, email Elizabeth O'Meara at <u>elizabeth@walthampton.com</u>.

Journeys on the Edge: Living A Life That Matters

My first book, *Journeys on the Edge: Living a Life That Matters* is now in its second printing. An Amazon bestseller in two categories, it was named as one of the Top 10 Non-Fiction books in 2013 by the Idaho Authors and Book Awards.

Somehow this little book has traveled to the far corners of the world; and although I wrote it with my own peeps in mind – those mid-career professionals who, though extremely successful, somehow find themselves in Dante's "dark wood" with no clear way out – the book has impacted the lives of young service men and women in the Middle east and senior citizens around the globe (as one 80 year old woman wrote, "seniors have dreams too!")

The message of *Journeys*: Live richly, fully, here, now, before the clock runs out.

Available on Amazon, at bookstores and on my website, www. walthampton.com.